The Grave Doug Freshley

THE GRAVE DOUG FRESHLEY™

A yarn about friendship, vengeance and not letting fatal head wounds interfere with your most solemn promises.

as revealed to **Josh Hechinger**
and depicted by **mpMann**

ARCHAIA ENTERTAINMENT LLC
WWW.ARCHAIA.COM

THE
A yarn about friendship, vengean
GRAVI

l not letting fatal head wounds interfere with your most solemn promises.

DOUG FRESHLEY™

as revealed to **Josh Hechinger**
and depicted by **mpMann**

Written by **Josh Hechinger**
Illustrated by **mpMann**

Published by Archaia

Archaia Entertainment LLC
1680 Vine Street, Suite 912
Los Angeles, California, 90028, USA
www.archaia.com

THE GRAVE DOUG FRESHLEY Original Graphic Novel. August 2011. FIRST PRINTING

10 9 8 7 6 5 4 3 2 1

ISBN: 1-932386-70-X
ISBN 13: 978-1-932386-70-7

Printed in Korea.

"bang."

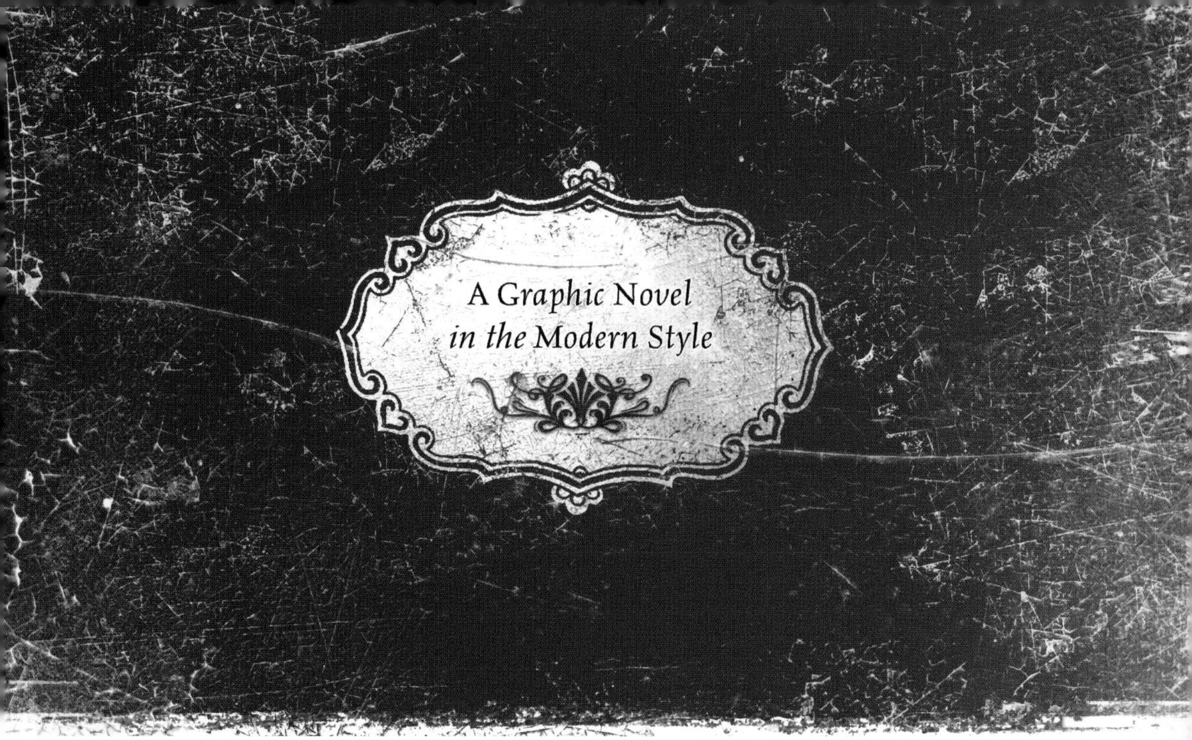
A Graphic Novel
in the Modern Style

TABLE OF CONTENTS

Foreword.....7

Chapter One: Once Upon a Time on the Range.....9

Chapter Two: Dead Man's Hand.....41

Chapter Three: Roadrunners and Coyotes.....73

Chapter Four: The Guns of Resolution.....105

Chapter Five: Grave Matters by Moonlight.....137

Unique Chapter Art depicted by (*in order of appearance*)

Anthony Peruzzo

Jorge F. Muñoz with Harry Myland

Scott Newman

Lea Hernandez

John Bivens

Time was, you could read the stories in a dime novel...

FOREWORD

So, then...

I get a message via Twitter from Josh, asking if I'd write the intro for this collection. Despite my complete lack of sleep, and much-too-full-schedule, I tell him "Sure no prob," asking for word count and deadline. Truth be told, I'm pretty jazzed to write it, because:

a) I've known Josh since he first stumbled onto Warren Ellis' The Engine forum, back when I was making my 'return' to comics.

b) I quite like the book. (A tale has to be damn good to overcome my dislike for all things cowboy related)

c) It's the first time anyone has asked me to write an introduction, and really my ego won't let me say no.

Also, I figure this'll be cake. ***The Grave Doug Freshley*** saunters and gallops with excellent pacing, humor, and an expressive style (both visually and in the telling) that feels both comfortable and unique at the same time. A more difficult thing to pull off than you might think. I admire both creators—Mann's work on ***Some New Kind of Slaughter*** and the fact that he's consistently chosen to do projects because they *challenge* him rather than doing the same genres and themes. And hell, I've worked with Josh as his editor on ***Comic Book Tattoo***. I watched him grow from the cocky kid Warren Ellis and I nicknamed "Marmot" (for his unfortunate facial hair) as he honed his chops, doing the work to transform from raw potential into skilled storyteller.

I'm a witty guy who gets paid for writing. Intro? Cakewalk.

Feeling especially brilliant, I spend a couple days writing this rather... involved... intro, using the 'Western' as an analogy (specifically, the HBO series ***Deadwood***) for Josh and MP's respective careers, their meeting on The Engine forum, how the 'new frontier' of comics was getting smaller... the unknown wilderness of comics feeling much less dirt trail, verdant forest, and icy rapids... replaced by clapboard sidewalks, formulaic architecture, and Rules For Your Own Good. How Warren, The Engine, and the creators involved felt like either the last true riders of the plains.

After three drafts, this analogy/narrative/intro was getting longer than the book itself and felt less and less like *"**Deadwood**"* and more and more like *"**John from Cincinnati**"* (except that I was a burned out hippie trying to explain Western imperialism to the cow skull named Rufus hanging from a macramé hanger in the living room). Here's an example:

"Those four-colour plains that once seemed so wide and open... hills full of multi-publisher gold waiting to be mined... well, they now seemed to be a-shrinking. The Engine and its inhabitants... be they homesteaders who'd cleared an acre of black and white pulp back in the day, or kids dressed in calico and seersucker arriving on the rutted muddy roads... meant to fight to keep the expanses wide. Young and old, these were folk who held that bootstrap pioneer spirit... drawn to the promise of a place where the frontier of comics was untamed and full of possibility, and a future largely determined by the confidence of the steel (pen nib) in your hand."

I mean really... when you find you've written something like that, you best just shut your damn piehole, hang your hat, and let the teller spin the tale.

Go on then, turn the page and get to the good stuff. The plains, honor, and justice await you...

—Rantz Hoseley
Orange County, CA
June 11, 2010

No. 1

"... the **Lord**, he ain't got a thing to do with it."

CHAPTER ONE

Once Upon A Time on the Range

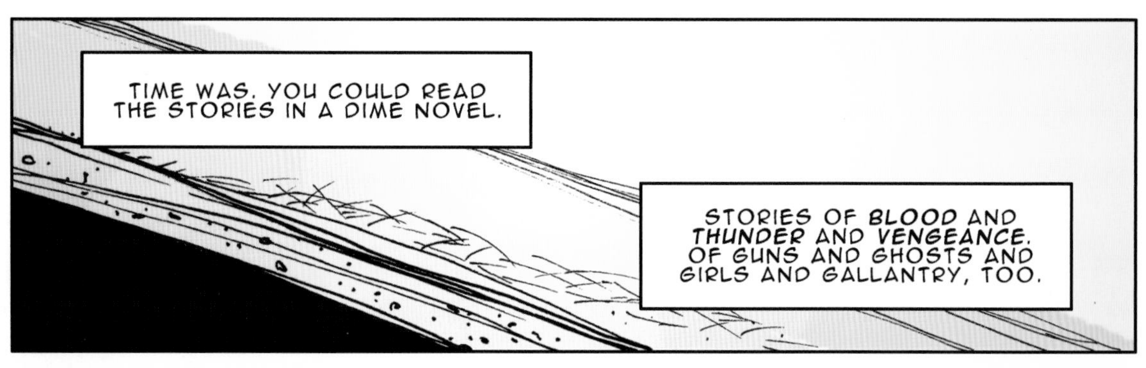

TIME WAS. YOU COULD READ THE STORIES IN A DIME NOVEL.
STORIES OF BLOOD AND THUNDER AND VENGEANCE. OF GUNS AND GHOSTS AND GIRLS AND GALLANTRY, TOO.

TALES OF GUNSLINGERS STARING DOWN A WILD LAND AND REACHING RESOLUTION WITH THEIR REVOLVERS.

AND EVERY ONE WITH SOME KINDA ***FANCY HANDLE***.

BUT AS A SMARTER MAN THAN MOST SAID:

"TRUTH IS STRANGER THAN FICTION."

AIN'T NO FANCY TITLES FOR THIS PAIR.

THE TALL DRINK OF WATER'S *DOUG FRESHLEY*. THE LITTLE ONE IS *BAT McNALLY*.

AND THEIR STORY JUST MIGHT BE THE STRANGEST OF ALL.

Chapter 1: ONCE UPON A TIME ON THE RANGE

a campfire yarn by: Josh Hechinger and mpMann

INCOMIN', DOUG!

FWEEEEEEEEEE!

WARK

GIT!

SWEETWATER
POPULATION:
DEPENDS
BOUNTIES ON THE DELANCEYS'RE UP AGAIN. HUH?

THWAK!

JUST THE BOSSMAN. HE'S UP FIVE GRAND FROM LAST WEEK.

NEVER MIND THAT NOBODY'S SEEN THE GUY.
???
WANTED
Dead or Alive
Ray Delancey
$15,000.00

SEEMS LIKE THEIR NEW THING IS RIDIN' UP ON A RANCH, SHOOTIN' ALL AND SUNDRY, AND MAKIN' OFF WITH THE CATTLE UNOPPOSED.

THINK I SEE IT.

WHERE?
DOWN TH'STREET THERE.

THEN HERE WE GO.
...HM.

KK-KK, HIYA!

HAHAHA!
GOTTA CATCH ME FIRST, OLD SON!
WOULD YOU COME HERE!?

WHULP!

WOULLLF!

UUUHHHH...

AW, DAMN.

YOU DONE RUNNIN' LIKE A FOOL?

HEALTHY EXERCISE IS FINE, BOY, BUT YOU'RE SUPPOSED TO BE STUDYING.
DUNWANNA.

FAIRLY CERTAIN YOU MEAN, "WHY YES, MR. FRESHLEY, SIR, I AM HAPPY TO ENRICH MY EDUCATION.
DUN E'EN KNOW WHAT HALF THAT MEANS.

WELL, THAT'S WHY YOU'RE GETTING AN EDUCATION.
PTOO.

DUN.
WANNA.

'WANT' AND 'NEED' ARE WORDS YOU'D DO WELL TO LEARN THE DIFFERENCE BETWEEN.

DUN SUPPOSE YE'D SHOW A POOR LAD LIKE MESELF SOME MERCY?

HAH?
HAH?

BROUGHT BACK YOUR BOY, MA'AM.

HOW FAR DID HE GET THIS TIME?
ABOUT A QUARTER MILE.

MY LITTLE BOY'S GROWING UP FAST.

BARTHOLOMEW? COME OVER HERE.

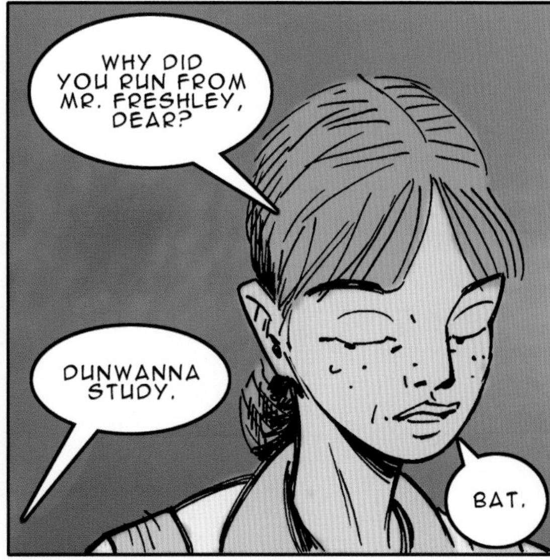
WHY DID YOU RUN FROM MR. FRESHLEY, DEAR?
DUNWANNA STUDY.
BAT.

DUN SEE A POINT'N BOOK LEARNIN', S'ALL.

NO POINT'N LEARNIN' 'BOUT SOME DEAD OLD KING,
O' HOW T'COUNT UP TO GOD KNOWS WHAT.

MMM...
I SHOULD BE HELPIN' DA SO AS WE CAN EAT. I SEEN YE 'N' HIM TAKIN' LESS FOOD SO I'VE A FULL PLATE.
OH, BAT!

I BEST SEE IF MR. McNALLY NEEDS ME.
MA'AM.

DO YOU KNOW WHY YOUR FATHER HIRED MR. FRESHLEY?
T'HELP WI'THE RANCH. N'CAUSE THEY'RE PALS FROM WAYS BACK.

THIS IS A SMALL RANCH. YOUR FATHER COULD HANDLE IT EASY.
BUT HE HIRED HIM TO TEACH YOU.

MR. FRESHLEY USED TO BE A SCHOOL TEACHER, LONG AGO.

YOUR FATHER WANTS YOU TO HAVE A FUTURE, AND THE FUTURE BELONGS TO EDUCATED MEN.

BUT I DUN HAVE TO LIKE IT.
NO DEAR, YOU DON'T HAVE TO LIKE IT.
WELL, OK.
SHANE.
YOU KNOW, YOUR GRAN USED TO HAVE DOUG DRAG YOUR FATHER TO SCHOOL AS A BOY...

AFTERNOON, DOUG.
BOY O' MINE'S BEEN A BIT O' TROUBLE?

NOT AT ALL. NOT AT ALL. FINE STUDENT.
UM-HM.

TO BE FAIR, CHASIN' PUPILS DOWN IS A PART O' BOOK LEARNIN', AYE?

IT'S HEALTHY EXERCISE. SOUND BODY FOR A SOUND MIND, AND ALL THAT.
HEH!

HEH-HEH!

HA-HA!

HEH!

THE ONE ON THE HORSE, FIRST.

FWEEEEEEEEEEEE!!!
BANG

YOU MISSED.

SWEET JESUS, WAS THAT-?
AYE.

GIVE IT HERE.

BANG!

UNF!

PQUEWHHH!!

AGH, DAMN...
LORDY, YOU'VE BEEN GUTSHOT.
Y'THINK?

I DON'T SEE WHERE THEY'RE HIDING...
NAH, LISTEN...

SHANE, C'MON, LET'S...
LISTEN T'ME, DOUG. YE MAKE SURE ME FAMILY'S SAFE, Y'FOLLOW?

YE'LL PERTECT ME BLOODY FAMILY!

GO, DAMN YE!

LET HIM GO.

TAZ'LL DO FOR HIM.

YE. I KNOW YE.

WE'VE MET?

SEEN THE POSTERS.

AH.

SORRY ABOUT YOUR FAMILY.

BLAM!

WHAT DID I JUST SAY ABOUT SHOOTING AT HIM?

BLAM!
BLAM!
YOO-HOO.

SEE YOU.

BLAM!

SKCH
SKCH

SHEEEEUT. MY GOOD HAT, TOO.

BLAM!
BLAM!
BLAM!

WHAT NOW, RAY?
ROUND UP THE CATTLE, TORCH THE HOUSE. SAME AS ALWAYS.

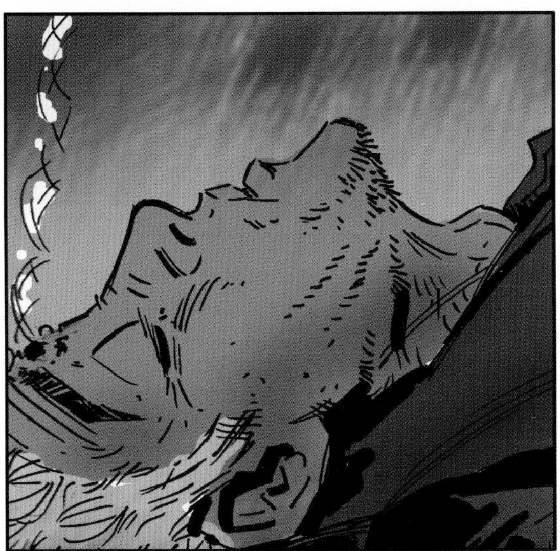

KAFF KAFF!

MA!
MA!

SOMEONE HELP!
ANYONE!
ANYONE?
...ANYONE?

BAT! WHERE ARE YOU, BOY?
OVER HERE!

THAT AIN'T NARROWING IT DOWN ANY.
THE KITCHEN.

DOUG!

HORSECRAP AND HELLFIRE!

DOUG... WHAT DO WE...

DOOOOO!

VRA-KOOOM!!
STAY HERE.

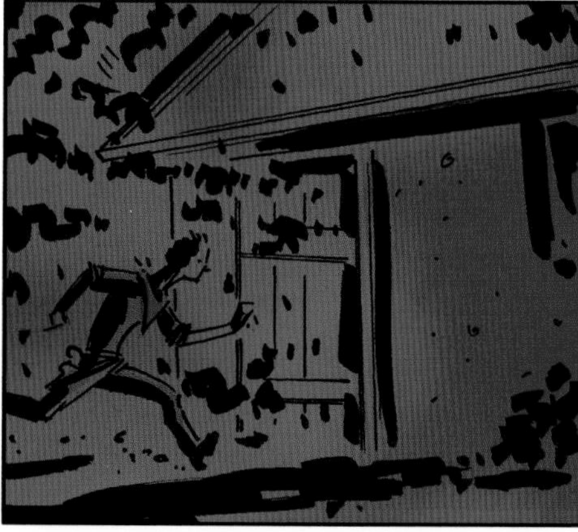

THEY'RE DEAD, AREN'T THEY?

I'M SORRY, BAT.

BUT I PROMISE YOU...

WE'LL MAKE THIS RIGHT.

SNIFF

TH'MAN... TH'ONE WHO SHOT ME MA...

I POKED OUT OF THE CABINET WHEN HE LEFT, Y'KNOW? I HEARD THE OTHER'UN COMIN', SO I WENT BACK IN--
BUT THE FIRST'UN HAD DROPPED THIS'N...

WHAT IS IT, BAT?

GARNER'S GREEN

COULD BE WHERE THEY'RE HEADING NEXT...

DOUG...

WHAT HAPPENED TO YER HEAD?

UM.

GARNER'S
GREEN
THIS THE PLACE?
SURE AS DEATH 'N TAXES.

HI-LARIOUS.
THANKEE.
I DO ME OWN BEST.

YOU STICK CLOSE, NOW. IF WE WEREN'T OUT FOR A RECKONING, I WOULDN'T LET YOU IN SPITTIN' DISTANCE OF A PLACE LIKE THIS.
FAIR ENOUGH.

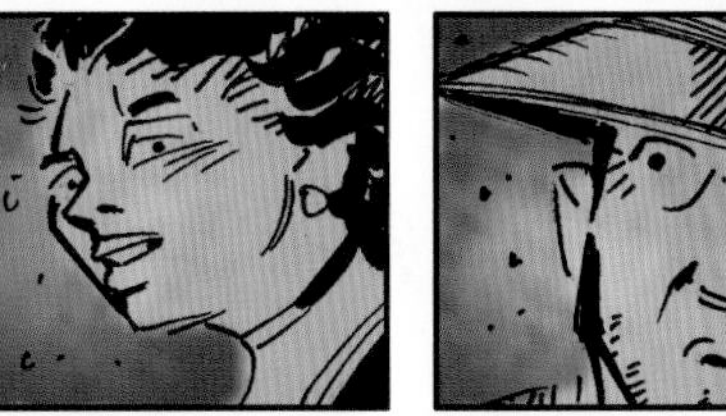

THERE.

AT THE TABLE.

NOW GENTS, I BELIEVE OL' LADY LUCK, WELL, SHE'S GOT A SOFT SPOT FOR ALL OF HER CREATURES...

BUT SOME MORE'N OTHERS, AND IT IS THE VAST MISFORTUNE OF Y'ALL TO BE SITTING AT THIS TABLE WITH ME.

YOU DON'T KNOW THE HALF OF IT.

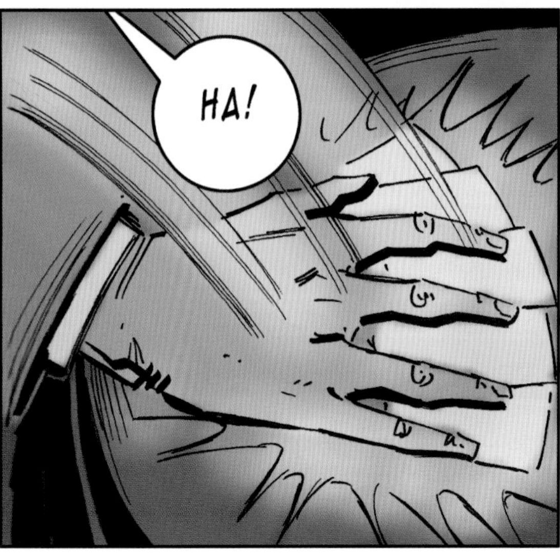
HA!

READ 'EM THROUGH YOUR TEARS AND LAMENTATIONS.

WHA--?

WELL HELL, FOLKS, IT'S JUST A FLUSH...

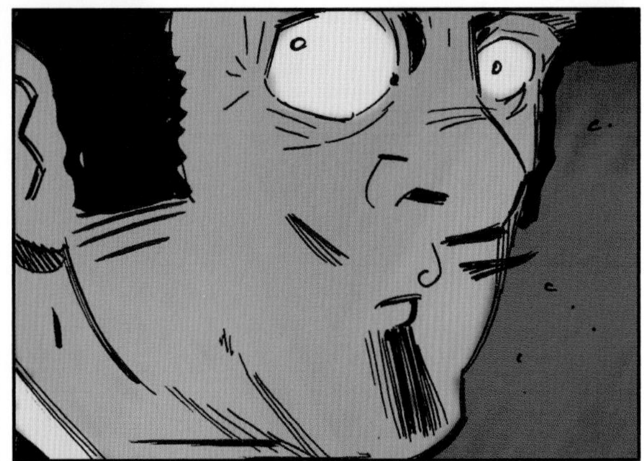

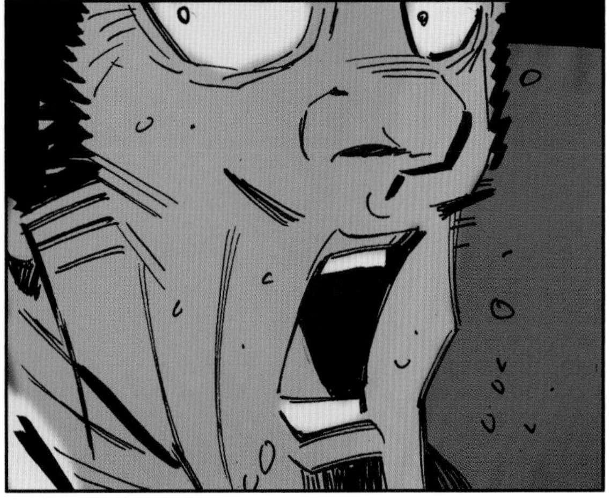

HOWDY.

LORDY...
IT CAN'T BE...

IT SURELY CAN...

AND THE LORD,
HE AIN'T GOT A THING
TO DO WITH IT.
COME 'ROUND AGAIN FOR
THE CONTINUATION.

No. 2

"... that last shot you and yours took? **Didn't take.**"

CHAPTER TWO

Dead Man's Hand

THE OLD WEST SHOOT OUT TENDS TO PICK UP A CERTAIN *MANLY DIGNITY* IN POPULAR FICTION.
THE INVOLVED PARTIES SQUARE OFF *FAIRLY*. FASTEST DRAW AND SUREST HAND MAKES FOR THE *VICTOR*.

WHICH IS, PRACTICALLY SPEAKING, A LOAD OF *ROAD APPLES*.
(THAT BEING A POLITE WAY OF SAYING *HORSECRAP*.)

IF ONE PLACED VALUE ON *BREATHING*, THE ELEMENT OF SURPRISE WAS KEY IN A GUNFIGHT.

IN THIS CASE, WHERE CONTINUED BREATHING AIN'T A CONCERN...
A DIFFERENT KIND OF SURPRISE IS A LOT MORE SATISFYING.
Chapter 2:
DEAD MAN'S HAND

YOU AIN'T TAKING ME, SPOOK!

POK

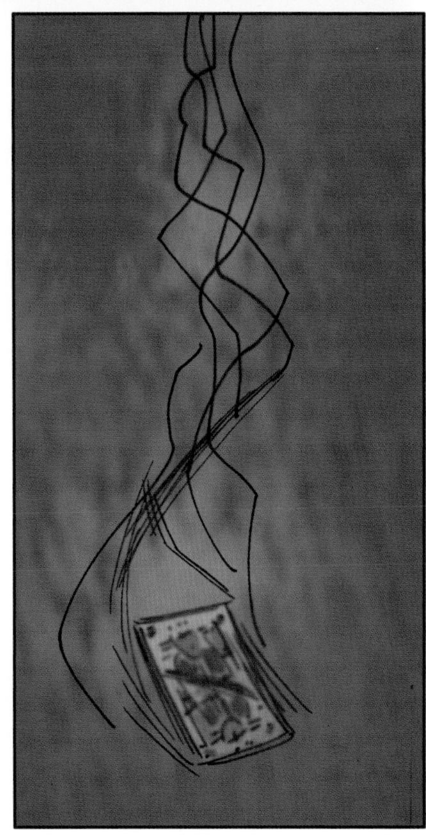

...WRONG SLEEVE.

AHA!

OH NO.
OH NO.
HE'S GOT A GUN.

AND I'LL USE IT! JUST YOU WATCH, HEAR!

YOU RECKON THAT'LL DO FOR ME?

CAUSE THAT LAST SHOT YOU AND YOURS TOOK? DIDN'T TAKE.

NOT THE FACE.

YOU KILLED THIS BOY'S MOTHER.
CLACK

BETTER ME THAN MY BROTHER, IF THAT COUNTS FOR ANYTHING.

NO.
NOT REALLY.

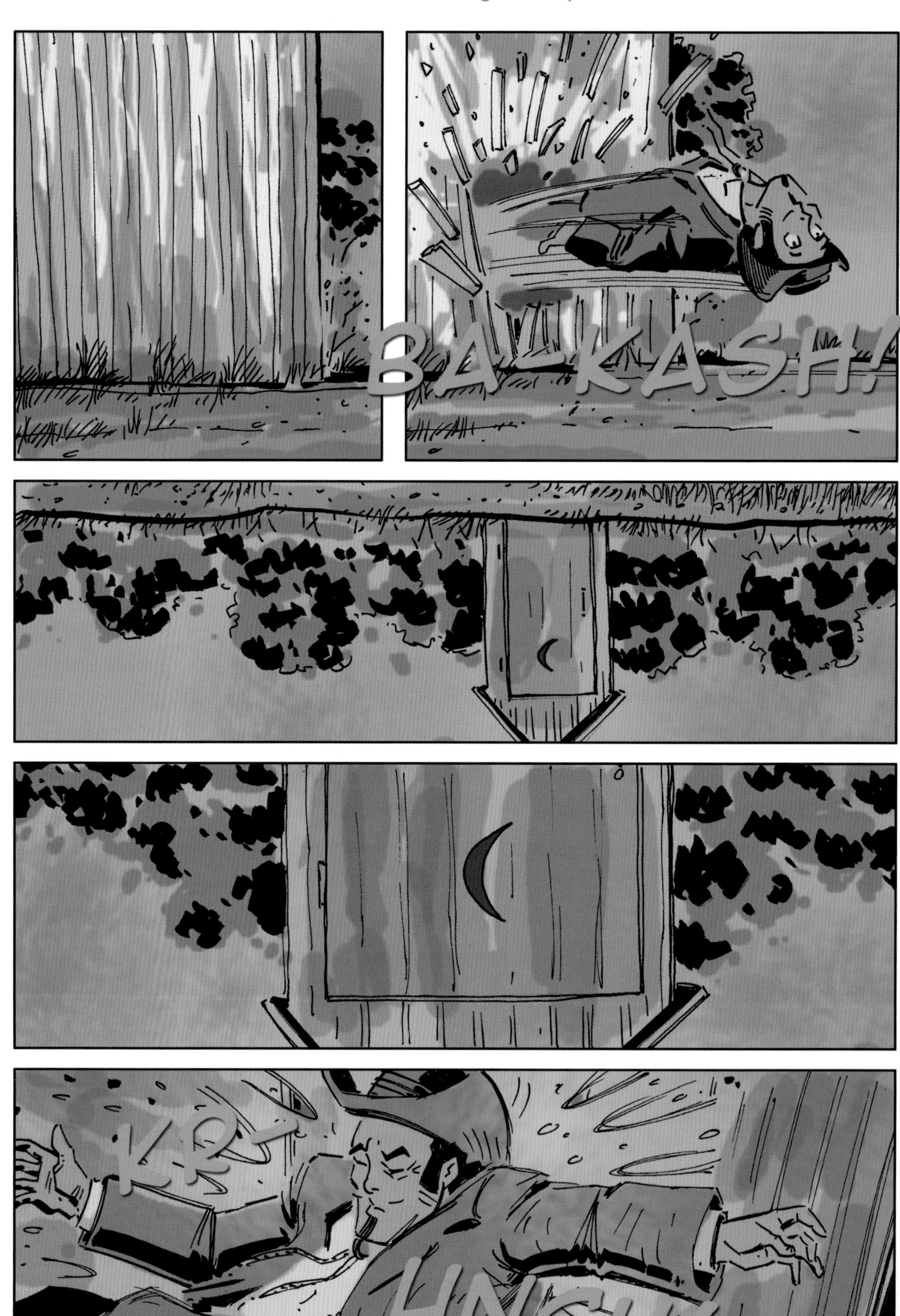
BA-KASH!
KR-
UNCH!

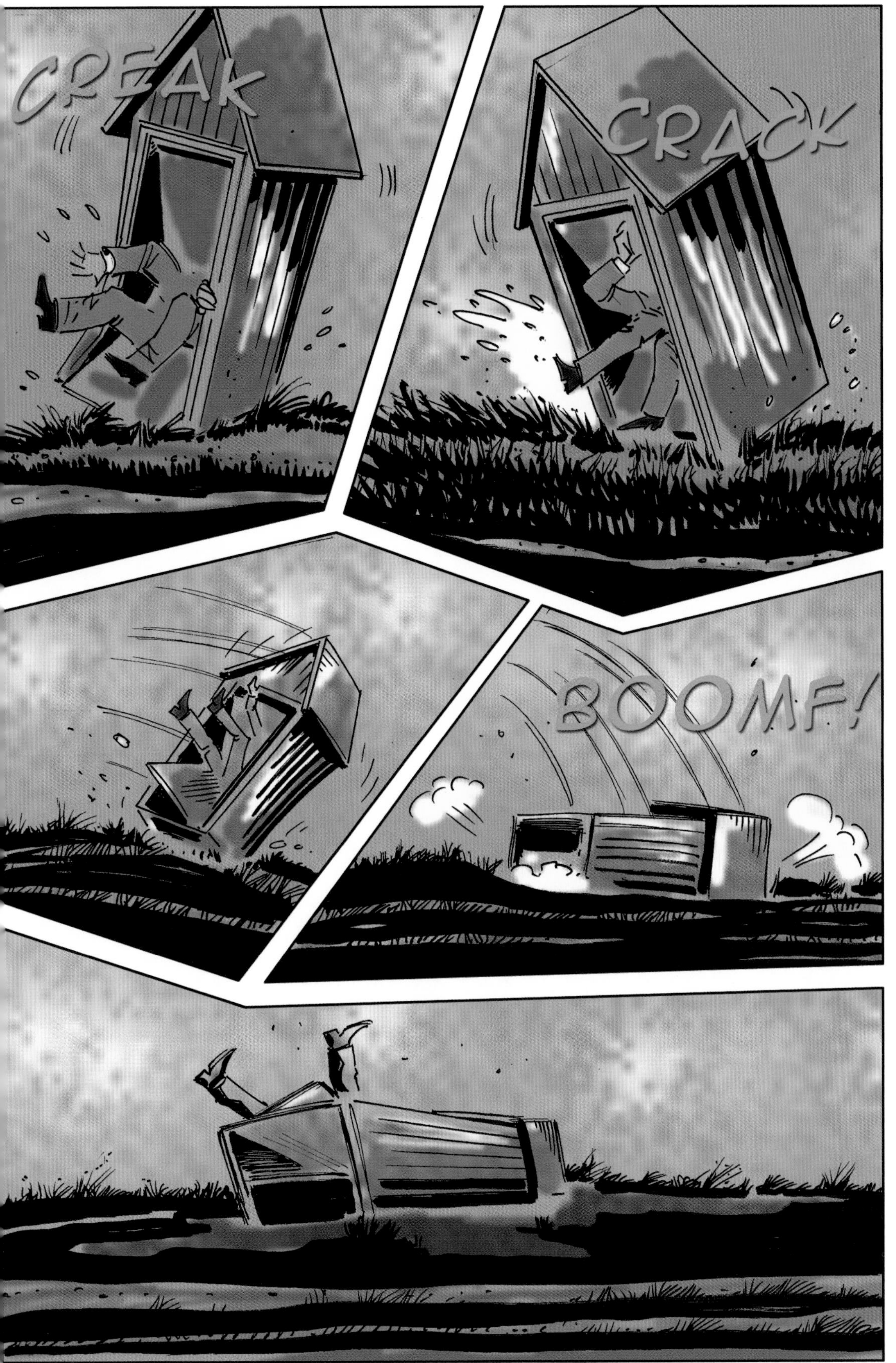
CREAK
CRACK
BOOMF!

WELL, SH--
WORDS LIKE THAT AIN'T CLEVER, BAT.

NOW DELANCEY...

WE'RE GONNA HAVE US SOME WORDS.

THUMP!
THUMP!
THUMP!
THWACK!
UHNFF!

SWAKKK!

SQUELCH
SQUELCH
SQUELCH
SQUELCH
SQUELCH
SQUELCH
SQUELCH
SQUELCH
SQUELCH
I SURELY DON'T KNOW NO BETTER WORD.

WHAT DO YOU FOLKS DO WITH CARD CHEATS?

ERMMM...

COME ON. BEST IF WE WERE ABOUT OUR BUSINESS.
HOW COME WE AIN'T KILLIN' HIM OUR OWNSELVES?
HE ISN'T WORTH IT. TOWN WILL SEE HIM TO JUSTICE.
WE'D JUST BE GETTING VENGEANCE. THAT'S A DIFFERENCE YOU NEED TO LEARN.
FAIR 'NUFF, BUT I THOUGHT...
UMM...

STRANGER, I THINK YOU'VE CAUSED US A FAIR BIT OF TROUBLE.
AND WE DON'T LIKE TROUBLEMAKERS ROUND THESE PARTS. THEY'RE TROUBLE.

DID YOU LISTEN TO THAT BEFORE YOU SAID IT. IN YOUR HEAD, I MEAN?

REDOUNAUT, IS WHAT IT IS.
REDUNDANT, BAT.
AH, THAT, AYE.

I THINK YOU BEST SLAP LEATHER.

BAT...
I'M JUST'N INNOCENT BYSTANDER, ME.

PTOOI

SPUT
PLOP!
BING!
BAM!
BANG!
BANG!
BANG!
BANG!
BANG!

HUUKK!

YOU DONE?

YEAH. I THINK YOU'RE DONE.

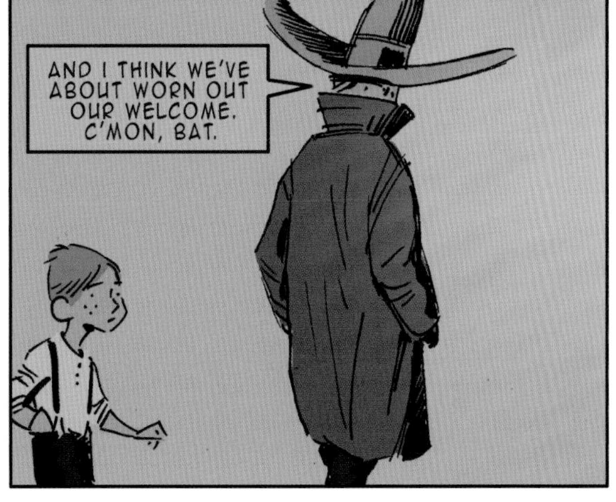
AND I THINK WE'VE ABOUT WORN OUT OUR WELCOME. C'MON, BAT.

MY BAR!

PYOW! PYOW

NOW *WHERE* THE... WHERE DID YOU GET THAT?
PYOW! TH' FLOOR, OF COURSE. FINDER'S KEEPERS'N ALL. *PYOW!*

GIVE THAT THING HERE BEFORE YOU SHOOT SOMETHING YOU SHOULDN'T.
AWW.

STILL HAVE SOME BUSINESS WITH US?
HEY!

AHUNH,
AHUNH...
WHEWW!

IF THAT'S THE CASE, IT'D BE IN YOUR INTEREST TO LET ME GET THE BOY CLEAR FIRST.

<HUFF>
AIN'T
<PUFF>
THAT
<WHEEZE>

AH-
HURMMM!

THAT CARD CHEAT... TURNS OUT HE WAS AN OUTLAW.
...WE KNOW.
AND THERE'S A REWARD.

AND...ER, WELL... I FIGURED I'D BEST APOLOGIZE FOR MY MEN'S CONDUCT JUST NOW.
SHOOTIN' YOU AND ALL, UNCALLED FOR.

WELL THAT'S VERY MANNERLY OF YOU, SHERIFF.

YOU AIN'T HURT NONE?
NO.
GOOD.

YOU, AH, YOU MIND IF I ASK WHY THAT IS?

Y'KNOW, WE HEAD BACK NOW, WE MIGHT STILL CATCH THE HANGING.

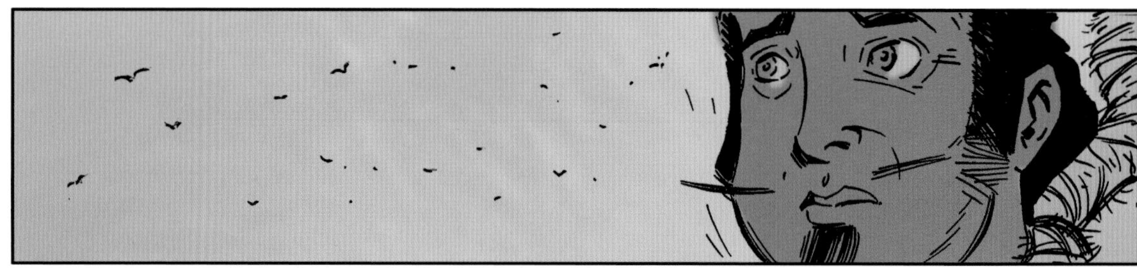

I DON'T SUPPOSE IT'D HELP MY CASE ANY TO CLAIM INNOCENCE?
THROW MYSELF ON YOUR GRACIOUS TOWN'S CHRISTIAN MERCY?

NOT REALLY, NO. BUT IF IT HELPS ANY, YOU GOT MY WORD ON A CLEAN BREAK.
US BEING TOO BUSY FIXING THE BAR TO WATCH YOU CHOKE.

SH- UNK!
WELL, PRAISE GOD FOR YOUR GENEROUS-
HURK!
WELL, HE'S THE REAPER'S PROBLEM NOW.

WELL, THAT'S DONE WITH.

THIS BOUNTY'LL GO A GOOD WAY TOWARDS REPLACING THAT COAT.
THUMP!

OFFER YOU BOYS SOME COFFEE?

NO. THANK YOU.

JUST RUN OUTTA THEM HOLES YE PUT'N HIM ANYHOW.
NOW, BE FAIR, I APOLOGIZED FOR THAT.

YOU AIN'T MISSING MUCH.

NOW, I THINK YOU BOYS GOT A STORY TO TELL, AND I WOULD SURELY LIKE TO HEAR IT.

BAT, WHY DON'T YOU GET THAT MONEY...

CHANGED TO BILL...
HUH, MOST MONEY THAT BOY'S SEEN IN HIS LIFE, I THINK.

I'LL BE TELLING IT. JUST...WASN'T SOMETHING THAT NEEDED REVISITING IN THE BOY'S PRESENCE.

HIM LIVING THROUGH IT WAS ENOUGH.

ME, I WASN'T SO LUCKY.

THAT'S A TERRIBLE STORY.
NEVER BEEN MUCH OF A STORYTELLER.

HA.
ANYWAY, I'LL THANK YOU FOR THE HOSPITALITY, AND BE ON MY WAY.

ONE LAST BIT OF HOSPITALITY I CAN EXTEND YOUR WAY.

REGARDING THE DELANCEYS.

HEARD THEY WERE RIDING FOR **KING HELL CANYON**. THERE'S A SALOON ON THE OTHER SIDE THEY USE TO REGROUP.

LEASTWAYS THAT'S WHAT I HEARD THEM TELL THE FOP BROTHER YOU HAD WORDS WITH.

WHICH WAY'S THE CANYON?
'BOUT THREE DAYS RIDE **SOUTHWEST**.

HE TOLD ME THEY WERE HEADING *NORTHEAST*, ABOUT *FIVE* DAYS RIDE.

JUST PASSING ON THE INFORMATION I HEARD.
I TRUST *YOU* MORE THAN *HIM*. MUCH OBLIGED.

ALRIGHT THEN, ALL KITTED UP. YE READY T'GO?

Y'LIKE THE HAT?

...BAT. DID YOU BUY ANYTHING ELSE?

RAN OUTTA MONEY.
THIS'S PLENTY, ANYWAY.

DUN SEE WHY I HAD TO RETURN ALL THAT CANDY.
HN.

D'YE NEED FOOD? NO YE DON'T. ME, I COULD LIVE OFF'O CANDY AN' NOTHIN' ELSE, EASY.
HN.

OH, YEAH, THIS'LL BE A FUN RIDE. TH' GRAVE DOUG FRESHLEY AN' SCARLETT BART MCNALLY, DARIN' AVENGERS.

"SCARLETT BART MCNALLY?" SOMEONE'S BEEN GETTING AT THOSE DIME NOVELS.
HIGH CLASS LITAMATURE, THOSE. BEATS THEM STUFFY BOOKS YE ALWAYS HAD.
SIDES, YE CAN'T ARGUE WE AIN'T LIKE SOMETHIN' OUTTA THEM BOOKS.
HOW SO?

HMM?

YE'RE THE WALKING DEAD, FR' ONE!
BAT... I AIN'T RIGHTLY SURE *WHAT* I AM.

I MADE A PROMISE TO YOUR PA TO KEEP YOU SAFE, IS ALL. I GOT A FEELING...

I THINK THAT'S WHAT'S KEEPING ME UPRIGHT.

NOW *GIVE* ME MY HAT BACK!

GIVE IT!

AND THEN WHAT?

...DON'T KNOW, BAT. I DON'T KNOW.

DOUG...

THANKS FOR LETTIN' ME KEEP MY HAT.

SO, WHERE'RE WE HEADIN', THEN?

THROUGH KING HE-HECK CANYON.
THEY'RE HIDING IN A SALOON ON THE OTHER SIDE.

CHING
THUNK!
CHING
KA-CHING

SPUT!
PTOO!

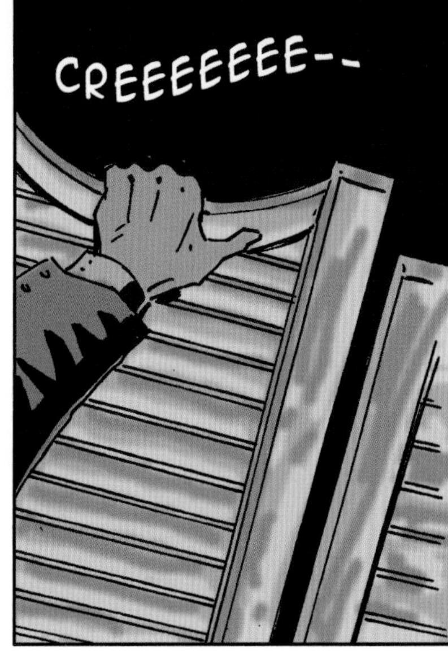
CREEEEEEE--

CREEEEEK

DON'T LOOK BACK...

WELL HOW-DY.
COME 'ROUND AGAIN FOR THE CONTINUATION.

No. 3

"... ain't no **running** from this..."

CHAPTER THREE

Roadrunners and Coyotes

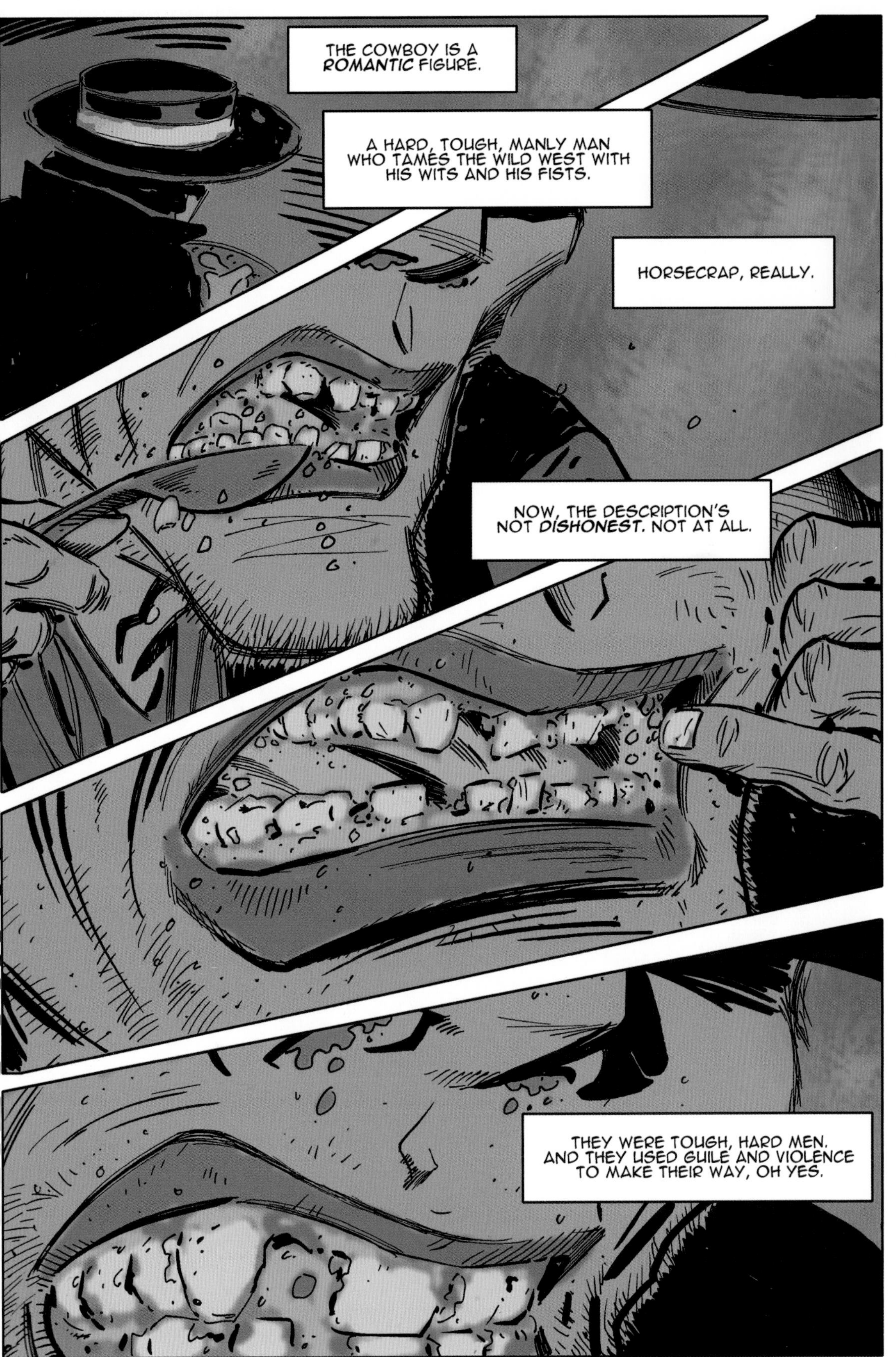
THE COWBOY IS A ROMANTIC FIGURE.
A HARD, TOUGH, MANLY MAN WHO TAMES THE WILD WEST WITH HIS WITS AND HIS FISTS.
HORSECRAP, REALLY.
NOW, THE DESCRIPTION'S NOT DISHONEST. NOT AT ALL.
THEY WERE TOUGH, HARD MEN. AND THEY USED GUILE AND VIOLENCE TO MAKE THEIR WAY, OH YES.

THE CONFUSING PART, OF COURSE, IS HOW THAT GOT TO BE CONSIDERED A GOOD THING.
Chapter 3:
ROADRUNNERS AND COYOTES

NOW THAT'S THE FACE OF A MAN WANTS T'GIMME A DRINK.

OR IZZIT MAYBE THE FACE OF A MAN WANTS HIS THROAT CUT?

ME, I GOT TROUBLE TELLIN'. SOMETIMES. WHEN I'M THIRSTY.
THUNK!

NOW, DID I ASK FOR BEER?

MAYBE I WANTED WHISKEY.

OR MAYBE I'M A WHOLESOME BOY, WANTED SOME MILK.
I-I-I-

LUCKY YOU, I WANTED BEER.

GLUG!
GLUG!

GLURRRP!

UNLUCKY FOR YA, YER BEER TASTES LIKE THE PISSA COMMON CATS.

TAZ.

KNOCK IT OFF. RAY'S WANTIN' A WORD.

NEED? NOPE. GONNA? YEP.

YEAH, RAY?

C'MON IN. ROCCO TOO.

SO, I GOT NEWS--

TELL ME THIS, IF'N YOU DON'T MIND...

YOU'RE LATE, AND YOU'RE ALONE, AND THERE HAD BETTER BE A DAMN GOOD REASON FOR BOTH.

OUTLAW HANGED

WHUT?

WEREN'T MY FAULT.

HEY NOW, NOW WAIT. IT WEREN'T.
FOOL GOT TURNED IN FOR GAMBLIN'! NOTHIN' I COULD DO, MY HONEST HAND TO GOD!

WELL?
...WELL WHUT?

YOU GONNA GO KILL THEM WHAT TURNED HIM IN, OR WHAT?

I'LL GET ON THAT, YEAH.

RIGHT NOW LIKE.
TAZ.

YEAH, SIS?'

YOU TAKE SOME ROAD AGENTS WITH YOU.
AND CLOSE TH' DOOR, THERE'S A DAMN DRAFT WAFTING YOUR MUSK OVER THIS WAY.

SLAM!
BRAT.
JACKASS.

HUHWAZZAT?

OH YEAH, THASSA COMFORTIN' NAME.
KING HELL CANYON

EASY PICKINGS. ON MY SIGNAL, WE BUSHWHACK 'EM.

BOSS, I THINK THAT'S THEM WERE LOOKING FOR.
DO TELL?

WELL, AIN'T THAT A HAPPY COINKYDINK.

BANG!
WHA--?

STAY DOWN UNTIL THERE'S A FINISH TO THIS.
D'YE THINK? ME, I WAS LOOKIN' T'GET SHOT.

NOW, UHF, AIN'T THE TIME FOR YOUR SASS, BOY.
AND DON'T GET TRAMPLED.
THUNK

NICE THING, RIGOR MORTIS MAKES FOR A STEADY...

SHOOTING...

HAND.
DAMNATION!

PLAN B, BOYS!

AIN'T NO RUNNING FROM THIS, DELANCEY.

YOU STAY PUT, BAT!

PUT YER BACKS INTIT!
--WEAK-ASSED BACKWATER DANDIES--

ALMOST!
ALMOST!

SON OF A--

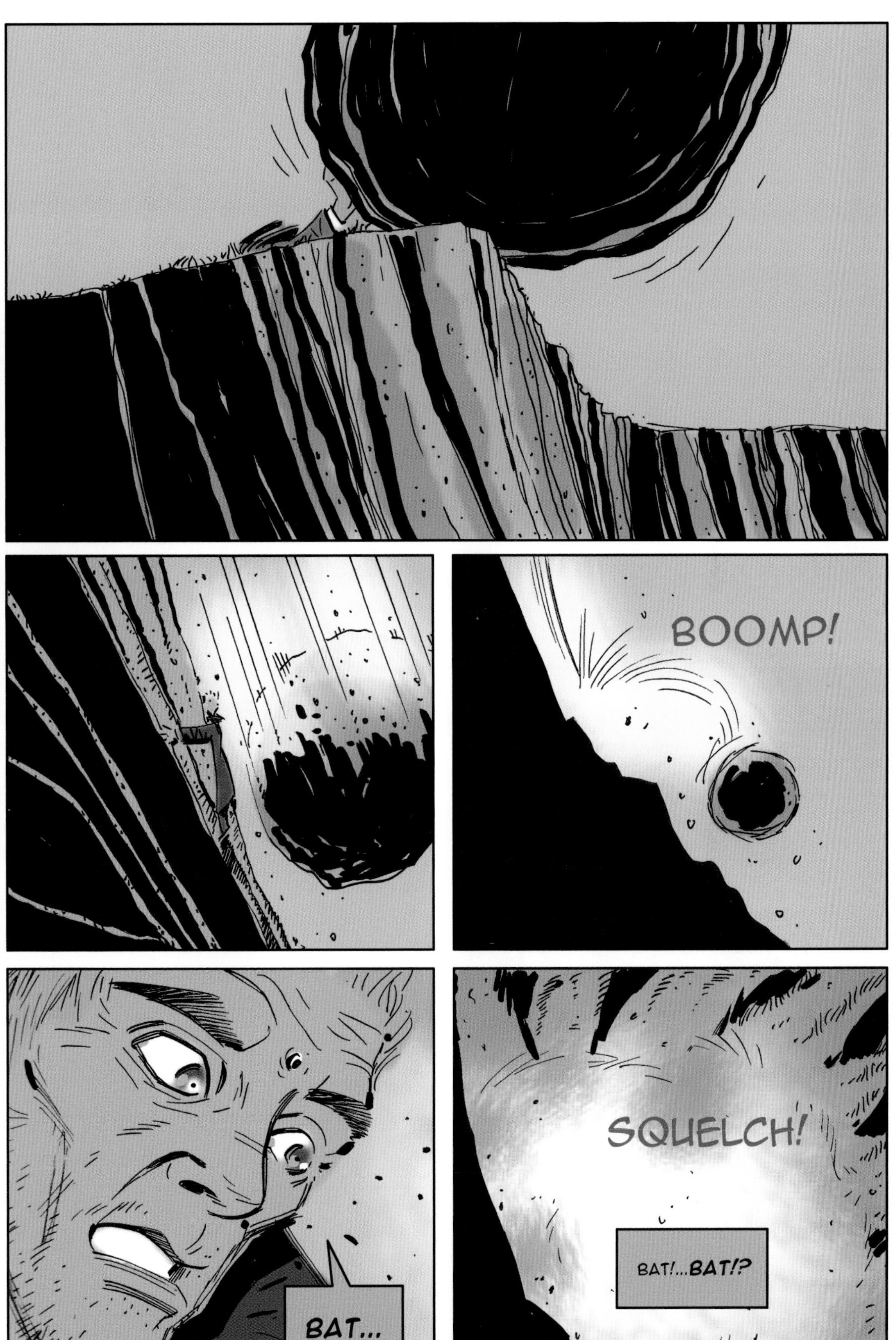
BOOMP!
BAT...
SQUELCH!
BAT!...BAT!?

>COUGH<
>COUGH<
M'FINE!

HORSE'S HAD IT THOUGH!

WHEWW!

AH, HELL, HE'S STILL COMING.

DOUBLE PAY FOR WHICHA YA DOES FOR THAT GREY-SKINNED SON OVVA WHORE

GET!

"STAY PUT," SAYS HE. FAT LOTTA GOOD THAT DID ME, DINNIT?

HE'S NOT LEAVIN' ME BEHIND, NOTTA CHANCE.

'N SECOND THOUGHT... URG...

HE... URG... MIGHTA BEEN ONTA SOMETHING.

N'ER TOO LATE T'TURN AROUND...

THEN AGAIN...

...THOUGHT I TOLD YOU TO STAY PUT.

YEAH, AN' THEN A BIG DAMN--
BAT.
DARN ROCK NEAR FELL'N ME. SO NUTS T'YER "STAYING' PUT" IDEA.

WHEW.

CLIMB ON.
WHY?

BECAUSE HE'S GETTING AWAY!

PARDON ME ASKIN'...
BUT HOW'RE YE PLANNIN' ON CATCHING' HIM, THEN?

HIS HORSE HAS TO STOP. I DON'T.

SILVER MINE
IT'S BEEN MINED, MIND

AIN'T NO POINT IN ASKING YOU TO MIND THAT HORSE, IS THERE?
NOPE.

THEN STAY CLOSE.

O'YEAH, THIS'LL NOT BE CREEPY A'TALL.
SHUSH, BAT.

NOW I RECALL CONFISCATING THAT A FEW WEEKS AGO.
CLEARLY, I STOLE'T BACK.

YOU ARE YOUR FATHER'S BOY FOR SURE.

UFF!
BAM!
BLAM
BAM!
THP
THP
BLAM!
P-CHOOO!
WOAHEY!

NO MORE OF THAT, DEAD MAN.
BAM
CRACK!

NOW, I DUNNO HOW YOU'RE ALIVE.
CLICK
DUNNO HOW MANY BULLETS IT'LL TAKE TO CHANGE THAT NEITHER.
GONNA HAVE FUN FINDIN' OUT, TRUTH BE TOLD.
THWAK!

I REMEMBER YOU. AND TH' NEXT ROCK'S GOIN' SOMEWHERE MEAN.
DON'T NEED NO GUN TO DO FOR YOU...

HEY! HEY!
OUHFF!
OKAY. OKAY. C'MON THEN, YOU MO--
POK!
CLANK! CHU-KUNK KSSSH
UFF!

NICE SHOT, BAT.

I DO ME OWN BEST.

ON THREE, THEN?
YEAH. I RECKON SO.

ONE...
TWO...
THREE!

KATTAKACHUTAKA-KATAKACHUTAKA

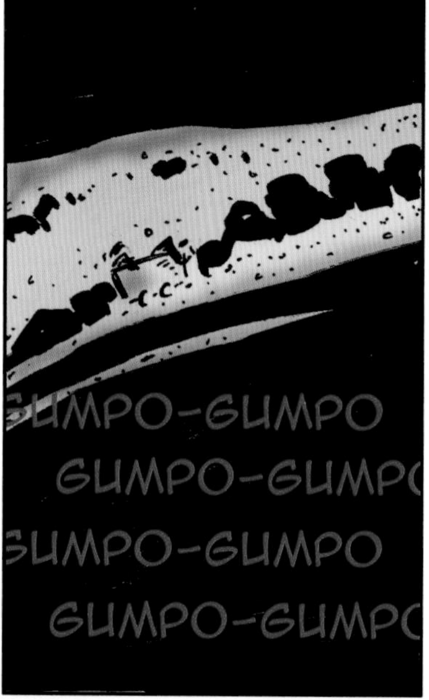
GUMPO-GUMPO
GUMPO-GUMPO
GUMPO-GUMPO
GUMPO-GUMPO

WHA--?
KATAKACHUTAKA

KU-CHUNG!

KREEEEEEEEEE!!

SON OF A--
VA-CHUNK!

THUMP

SAME T'YE.
BASTARD.
HEY NOW.
LANGUAGE.

BUT HE WAS!
HE WASSA RIGHT--

YEAH,
HE WAS.

C'MON. NOTHING TO KEEP US HERE.

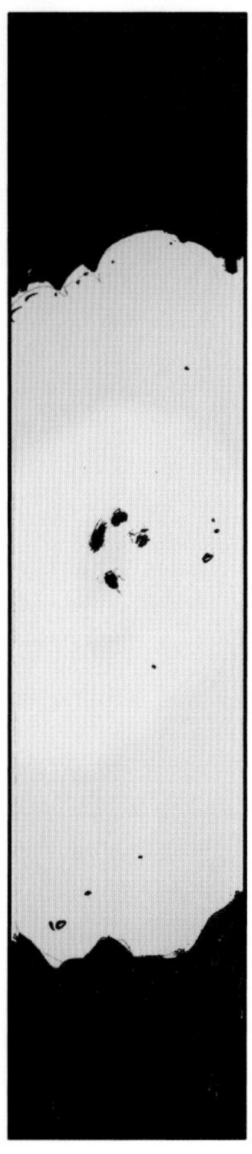

SEEMS LIKE I'M PICKING UP AFTER YOU AGAIN.
WE WON'T BE HAVING WITH THAT MUCH LONGER.

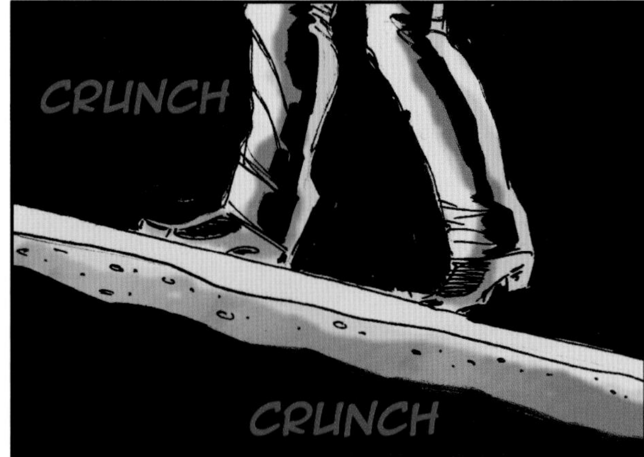
CRUNCH
CRUNCH

YOU MARK ME, WE'LL FINISH OUR BUSINESS

AS SURE AS I AM THE REAPER.
COME AROUND AGAIN FOR THE CONTINUATION.

SILVER MINE
It's been mined, mind.
NEWMAN 2010

No. 4

"**Hobbies**. Everyone's got 'em."

CHAPTER FOUR

The Guns of Resolution

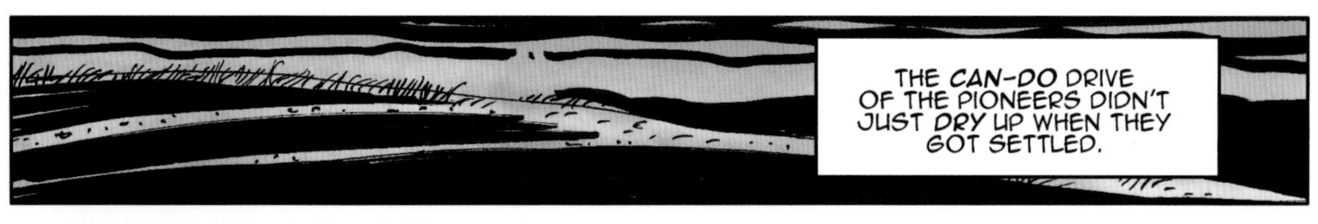
THE CAN-DO DRIVE
OF THE PIONEERS DIDN'T
JUST DRY UP WHEN THEY
GOT SETTLED.

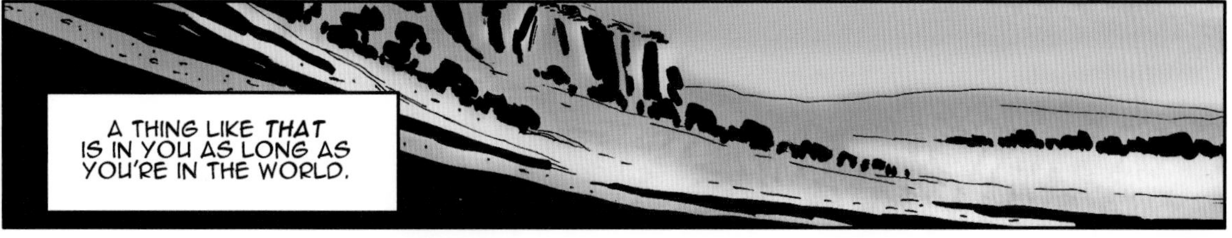
A THING LIKE THAT
IS IN YOU AS LONG AS
YOU'RE IN THE WORLD.

KLOPPATA-KLOPPATA-KLOPPATA

SO IT HAD TO FIND
OTHER OUTLETS. WORKING
THE LAND. RAISING A TOWN.
DIGGING FOR GOLD.

SOMETIMES,
JUST LIVING WAS
ENOUGH.

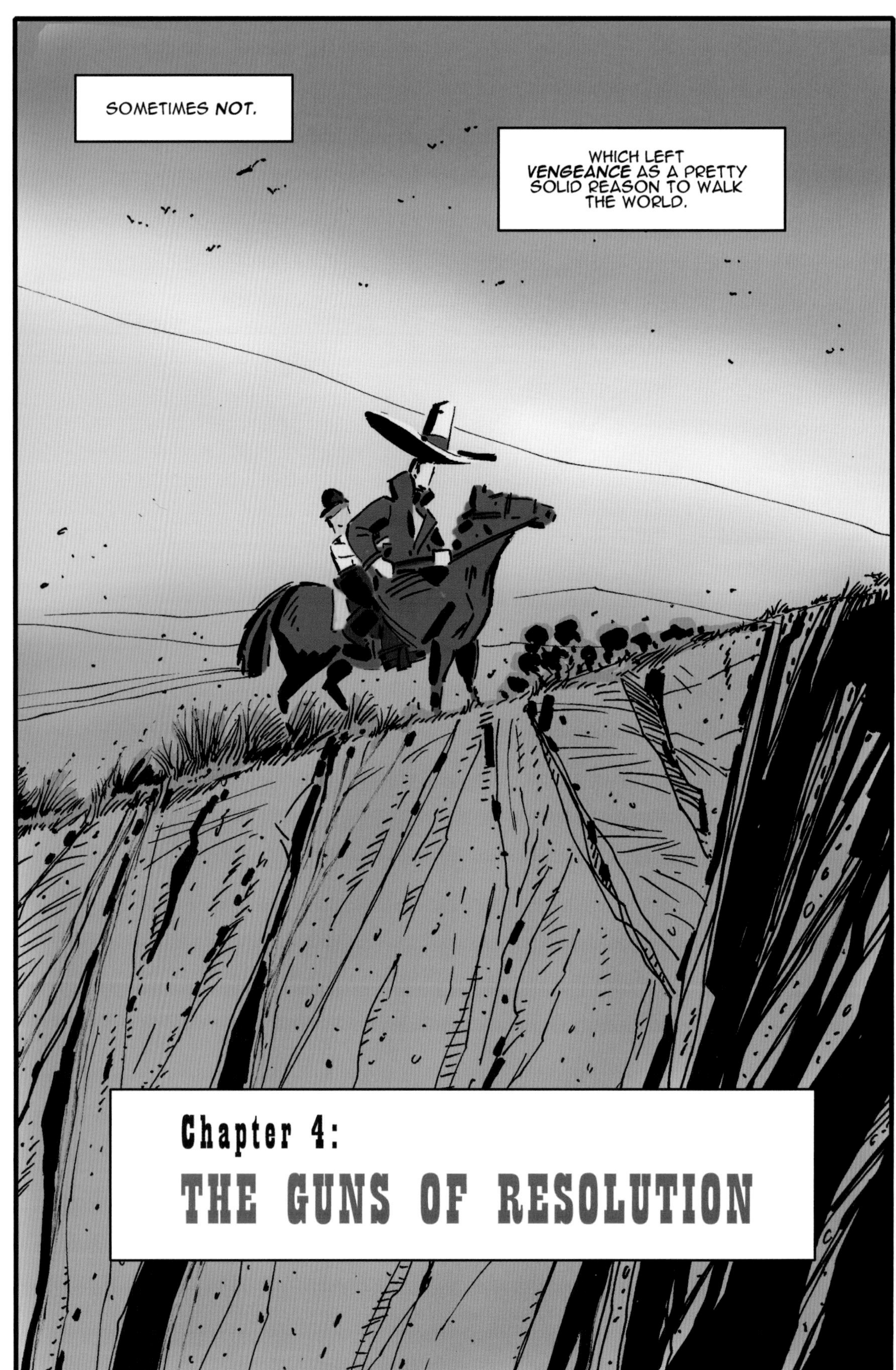
SOMETIMES NOT.
WHICH LEFT VENGEANCE AS A PRETTY SOLID REASON TO WALK THE WORLD.
Chapter 4:
THE GUNS OF RESOLUTION

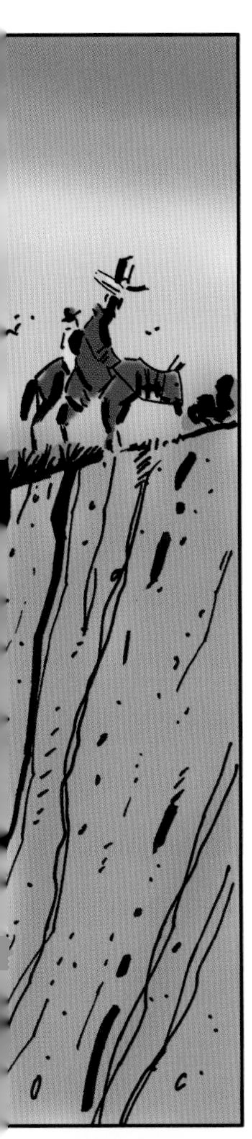

YE'VE NO CLUE WHERE WERE GOIN', DO YE?
NOPE. NOT AS SUCH.

I THINK I SEE A ...FARM? WE CAN MAYBE ASK'EM WHERE WERE AT.
WORTH A SHOT.

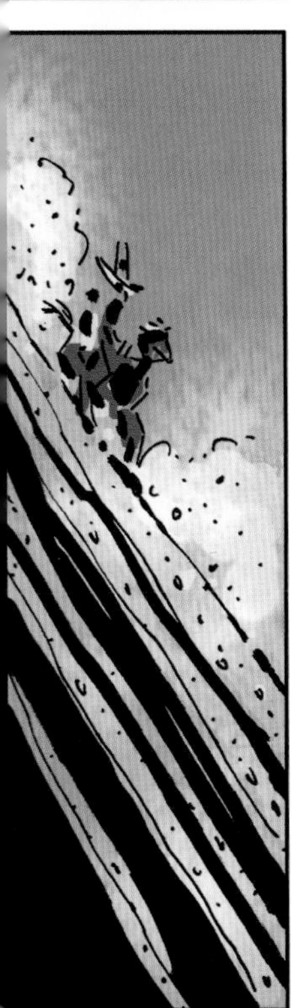

OH.

AW, NO...

STAY BY THE HORSE.

B-BUT...
STAY BY THE HORSE.

D'L SEAS...

WHAT?
'T...S...D'L SEAS...
ONE MORE TIME?
DILL...ANT... SEAS...

MAYBE YOU BEST NOT TRY TO TALK IN YOUR STATE, SIR.

DELANCEYS, Y'DAMN FOOL! THEY WENT--

NOOOORTH...
YOU REST EASY.

I'LL BRING THEM WHAT DID THIS TO ACCOUNT.

YE--
YE GIT ANY DIRECTIONS, THEN?
YEAH.

NORTH.

CLINK
HEH, HEH
HA!

THWAK!

SNARL
CLANK
GRUMBLE
HMMF

CHEERY PLACE, INNIT?
DON'T SASS THE REGULARS, BAT.

YEAH?
THE DELANCEYS. WHERE ARE THEY?

BOYS?

I'M SAYIN' THIS ONLY IN THE HOPE THAT YOU'RE GONNA KILL THEM, MIND...
ALREADY DONE FOR TWO OF THEM.

OH. WELL THEN...

"YOU RIDE OUT ABOUT FIVE MILES NORTH, TAKE A LEFT TURN AT THE TREE THAT LOOKS LIKE A ROOSTER, GO ABOUT THREE MILES, AND THERE YOU GO."
THIS'S IT, THEN?
YEP.

I'M LETTING YOU COME ALONG ON THIS FOR TWO REASONS.
AN' THOSE'D BE?

THEY WERE YOUR PARENTS, AND YOU DESERVE TO SEE THIS THROUGH.

I'M TRUSTING YOU TO STAY OUT OF TROUBLE WHEN I TELL YOU TO.
...RIGHT YE ARE.

GIVE 'EM THIS... WOULDNA PEGGED *THAT* FOR A BANDIT HIDEY-HOLE.

QUIET, NOW.

CREAK!

BUSHWHACKERS!

THWAK!

GET OUT OF HERE, BAT!

RAY'S GONNA PITCH HELL OVER THAT HOLE'N THE WALL...

...HOLD ON!

THE KID?

HMM.

I'M COMIN' FOR YA! BELIEVE IT!

ERRP!

KRASH!
UUFF!
HAH!
YOU'RE THE ONE'S BEEN GOING AFTER US, HUH?
THWAK!
CAN'T SLIP MUCH BY YOU, CAN WE?

MEANWHILE, BACK AT THE RANCH...

WHA'S THIS?

EW, GIRL STUFF.

WAIT! GIRL STUFF?

SNIFF

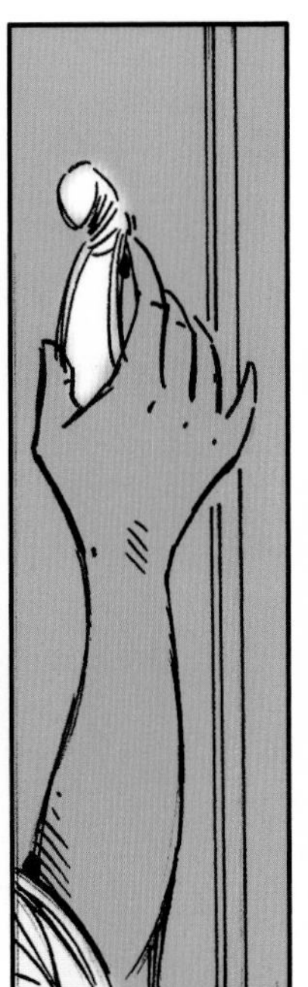

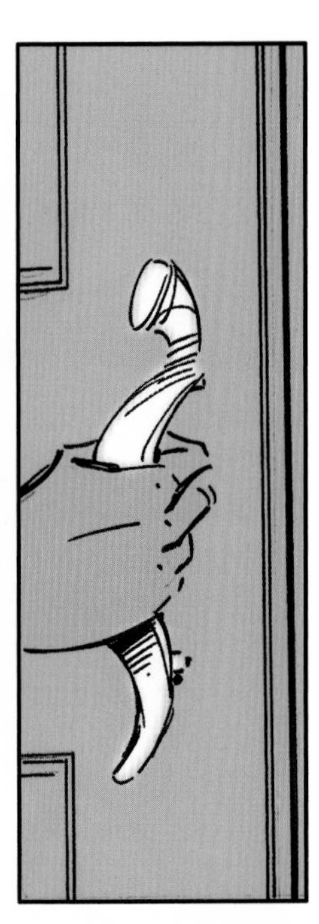

AH--

--HUH?

ARE THE
BAD MEN
GONE?

WELL. ME FRIEND'S GOIN' ROUND WITH ONE O' 'EM DOWNSTAIRS.
FISTICUFFS? HOW HORRIBLE!
WHAT WERE YE DOIN' IN TH' CLOSET ANYWAY?
WHY, I WAS HIDING FROM THOSE *HORRIBLE* BANDITS.

KTHUNK!

HAHF. HAHF.

WELL, I THOUGHT I'D PUT YOU DOWN.

SHOULD'VE KNOWN BETTER THAN TO TURN MY BACK...

ON A MAN WITH A PITCHFORK.

WELL?

UMM... YOU AIN'T DEAD.

NOOO.
I JUST AIN'T GETTING ANY DEADER.

THWAK!
HEY!
THERE'S MY HAT.

UFF!
THWAP!
MUCH BETTER.

THIS THING...

CAN'T REACH...
THUK!

THWAP!

ANNOYING...
THUNK!

ER, DOUG?

SHE HAD FEMININNY WILES.
AND A GUN.
THAT, TOO.

AND YOU ARE?
RACHAEL DELANCEY.
THE LITTLE SISTER, HUH?

THE BOSS.

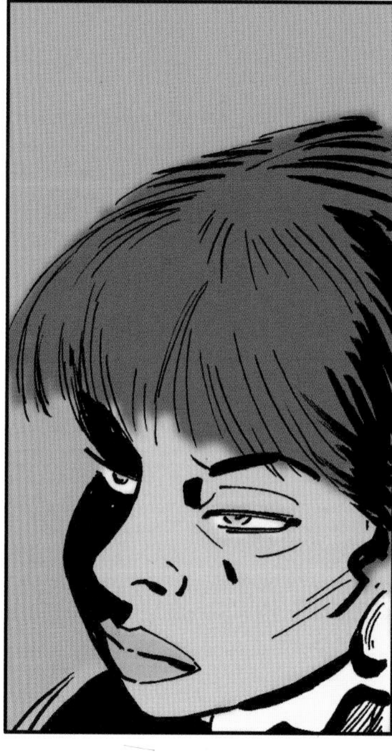

DOUG FRESHLEY, INCIDENTALLY.

I DON'T RECALL ASKING.
DON'T RECALL YOUR FACE, EITHER.

AND YOU HAVE ONE I RECKON I'D RECOGNIZE.

Y'KILT ME MA AND PA!

THWAK!
YEAH?

I DO THAT, SOMETIMES.

KILL FOLKS,
I'M SPEAKING OF.

I STEAL CATTLE AND BURN HOMES AND DO WHATEVER WORSE DEEDS COME UP IN THE PROCESS OF DOING BAD ONES.

I ALSO DO NEEDLEPOINT AND COLLECT POSTCARDS.

HOBBIES, EVERYONE'S GOT 'EM.

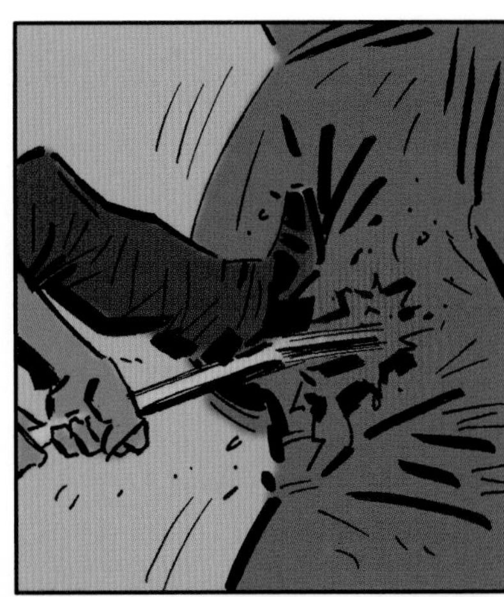

AH!

BANG!
BANG!
BANG!

GGGH...

I THINK YOU BEST HAND BOTH GUN AND BOY OVER, DELANCEY.
YOU GO TO HELL, DEAD MAN.

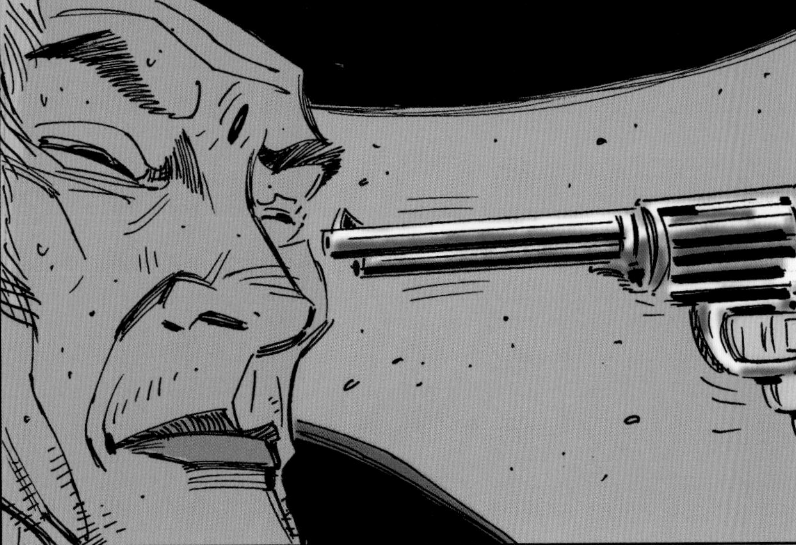

BOOM!
CLICK

YOU BLOCKED THE BARREL?
YEAH.

THAT'S...WELL, PRETTY TRICKY OF YOU, BAT.
I DO ME OWN BEST.

SO,,,S'OVER.
YEP.

...I DUN FEEL ANY BETTER 'BOUT ME MA 'N' PA.
NO, I RECKON NOT.

SO... NOT THAT I'M COMPLAININ' MIND, BUT YE'RE STILL HERE.

YEAH, BEEN WONDERING ABOUT THAT MYSELF.

DON'T LOSE ANY SLEEP OVER IT.

BECAUSE I PROMISE YOU DOUG FRESHLEY, IT WON'T BE MUCH OF A CONCERN FOR LONG.
...BEG PARDON?
COME 'ROUND AGAIN FOR THE CONCLUSION.

TNT
LEAHERNANDEZ
2KX
7.16

No. 5

"Don't sass the **Grim Reaper**, boy."

CHAPTER FIVE

Grave Matters by Moonlight

TO THOSE OUT WEST, DEATH WAS A NIGH-CONSTANT COMPANION.

IT WAS IN THE SUN AND THE DIRT.
OR IN THE GLINT IN A HARD MAN'S EYES.

DEATH WASN'T PARTICULARLY CHOOSY ABOUT ITS COMPANIONS.
YOUNG OR OLD, GOOD OR BAD, SO ON AND SO FORTH. THE PALE RIDER RODE HERD ON EVERYONE SOONER OR LATER.

ON THE BRIGHT SIDE, DEATH USUALLY HAD THE GOOD GRACES TO STAY METAPHORICAL.
TODAY, THAT AIN'T SO MUCH THE CASE.
Chapter 5:
GRAVE MATTERS BY MOONLIGHT

HOWDY, BOYS. I'M DEATH.

THE PALE RIDER? THE LAST SUNSET? THE GRIM REAPER HIS OWN SELF?
YOU BOYS FOLLOWING ME?

RUNNING IS NOT AN OPTION HERE.

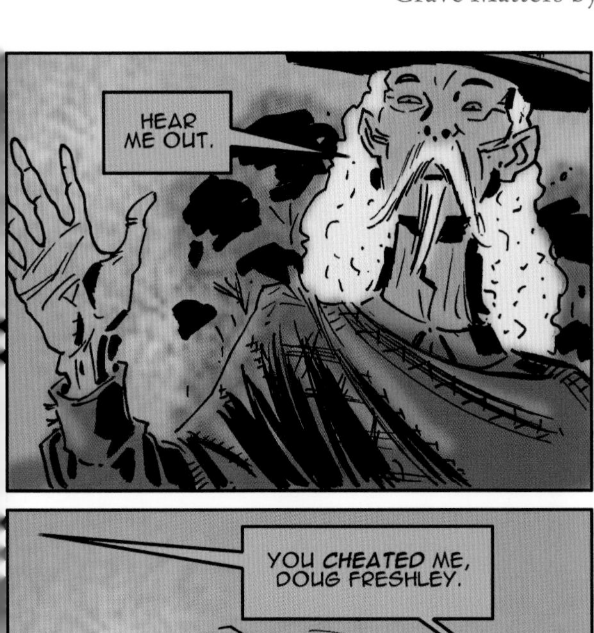
HEAR ME OUT.
YOU CHEATED ME, DOUG FRESHLEY.

IT'S BEEN DONE BEFORE, MIND. USUALLY BY TOUGHER MEN THAN WHAT YOU WERE.

BUT YOU TOOK IT... FURTHER THAN MOST.

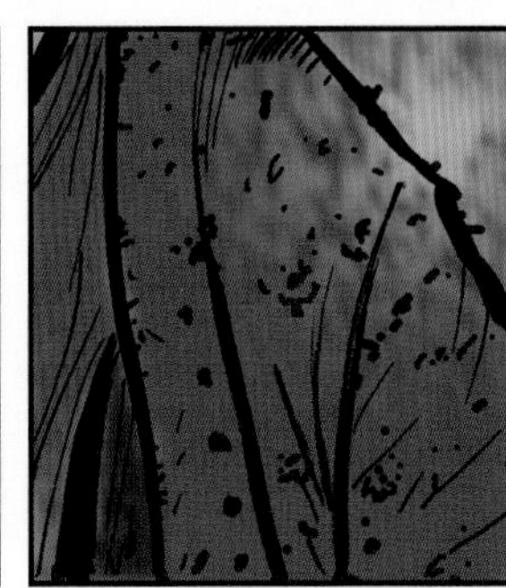

I MADE A--
I DON'T CARE. YOU'RE PAST DUE, IS THE POINT I'M MAKING HERE.

NOW, THERE'S TWO WAYS WE CAN SETTLE THIS.

I CAN JUST SHOOT YOU HERE, QUICK AND PAINLESS, GUARANTEED.
CLICK

OR YOU CAN DRAW AGAINST ME, IN WHICH CASE...WELL, SEE THE FIRST OPTION.
CLICK

EITHER WAY...BANG. YOU'RE DEAD, AND ALL THE WAY, THIS TIME AROUND.
BANG!

MAKE YOUR CHOICE.

YE CAN'T *HAVE* HIM!

I'LL DRAW AGAINST YE, REAPER MAN.

AND I'LL BLOW A HOLE CLEAN THROUGH YE AFORE YOU TAKE ME FRIEND.

I'VE NO BUSINESS WITH YOU TODAY, BAT. YOU'VE A LOT OF RIDING YET TO DO.
BAT! DON'T SASS THE GRIM REAPER, BOY.

THERE'S A CEMETERY SEVEN MILES WEST FROM HERE.

YOU COME THERE, WITH YOUR ANSWER, AT HIGH MOON.

AND WE'LL FINISH OUR...

BUSINESS.

...HUH.

SHOULDA GIVEN HIM ONE'N TH' NADGERS AFORE HE LEFT. SMOKE O'NOT.
I'M...NOT SURE HE HAS THOSE, BAT.

WORTH A SHOT.
C'MON. THOSE DELANCEYS AIN'T GONNA BURY THEMSELVES.

YOU COULD HELP.
AIN'T SWEATIN' T'GIVE THEM PROPER BURIAL, AN' THAT'S A FACT.

SIDES, AIN'T LIKE YE GET WORN DOWN ANYMORE.
FAIR POINT.

THINK WE SHOULD SAY ANY WORDS?

"GOOD RIDDANCE" ?

GOOD ENOUGH.

THO OO INIT EEDH T'EA?
SWALLOW, THEN TALK. YOU KNOW BETTER THAN THAT.

GULP.

THOUGHT YE DIDN'T NEED T'EAT ANYMORE.
ALWAYS PROMISED MYSELF I'D NEVER DIE ON AN EMPTY STOMACH.

YE AIN'T FIXIN' T'DIE THOUGH... RIGHT?

DIE MORE, ANYHOW. YER NOT INTENDIN' T'GET DEADER'S THE POINT I'M TRYIN' TO MAKE.

DON'T SEE HOW I CAN OUTDRAW DEATH, BAT.

WHICH AIN'T TO SAY I WON'T TRY.

DON'T YE WORRY. I'LL THINK OF SOMETHING.

GULP

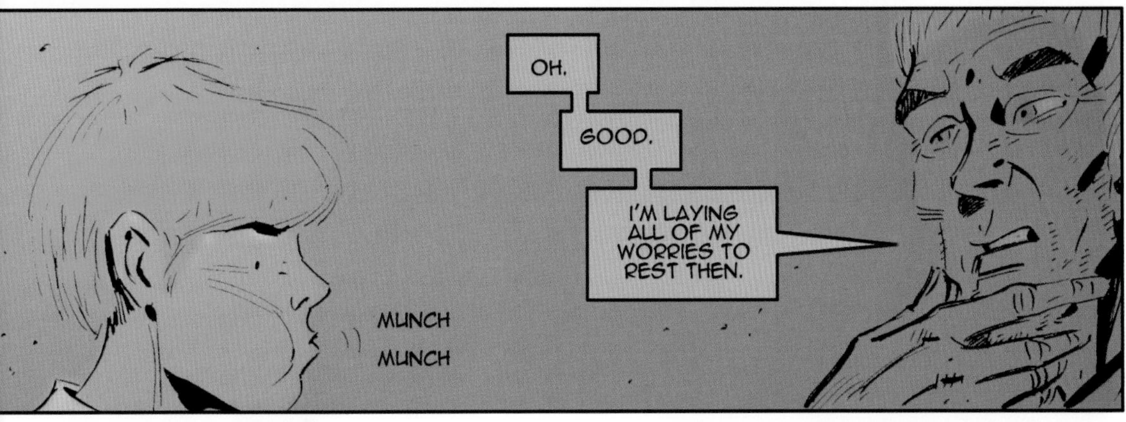
OH.
GOOD.
I'M LAYING ALL OF MY WORRIES TO REST THEN.
MUNCH
MUNCH

ULP!

WHAT TIME'S THIS 'HIGH MOON', THEN?
Y'KNOW, I DON'T RIGHTLY KNOW.

I KNOW HOW
TO FIND OUT.

ANH-HANH!

AUGUST... 2ND, 1876
SAYS 10:15. HUH.

OUT TO BE MIDNIGHT, SEEMS LIKE.
WHY'S THAT?

DRAMA. LIKE THE DIME NOVELS.

IT'S PAST YOUR BEDTIME, EITHER WAY.

LIKE
BAT!
IT IS!

IF'N YE'LL EXCUSE ME, I'VE GOT TO COME UP WITH A DARIN' PLOT T' SAVE YE!

EXPECTIN' ME T'SLEEP WHEN YE'VE A SHOOT OUT WITH T'GRIM REAPER.
HA! BAH, I'D EVEN SAY!

HERE
WE GO.

...DOUG?

SON OF A--
OOE~OOE~OOE~OOOOOOOOO

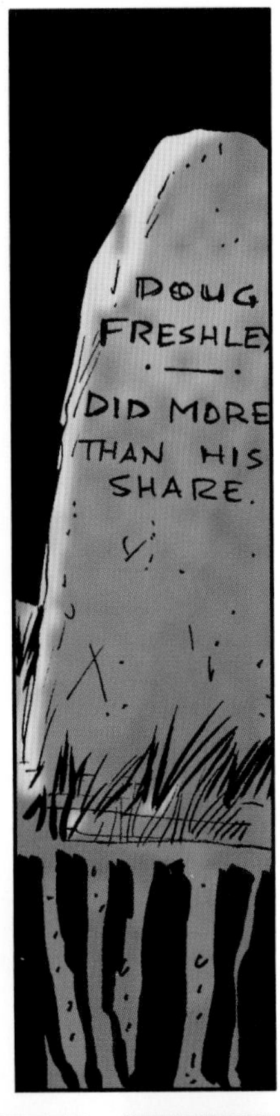
DOUG
FRESHLEY
DID MORE
THAN HIS
SHARE.

NICE TOUCH.

I DON'T HAVE MUCH HUMOR, BUT A LITTLE KINDNESS SEEMS TO BE APPRECIATED.
PRETTY SURE OF YOURSELF, AREN'T YOU?

RECKON I'VE REASON, DON'T I?

RECKON SO.

IT'S TIME.
WHAT'S YOUR CHOICE?

WHERE IS IT?

I THINK YOU AND I HAD BEST DRAW.

STAND THERE. NEXT TO, NOT IN.

DOU
FRESH
DID M
THAN M
SHAR

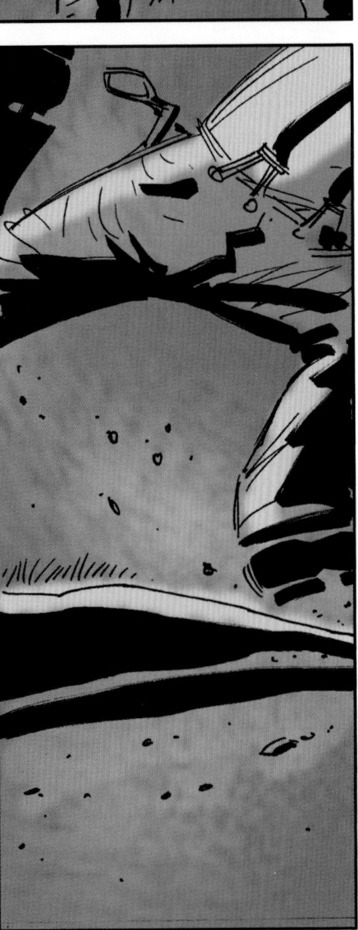

WHEN YOU'RE READY.

WHAT ABOUT BAT?

THE BOY'LL HAVE TO BURY YOU.

THAT'S THE EXTENT OF MY IMPOSITION ON HIM.

YOU'RE A CRUEL
MAN, Y'KNOW THAT?

I'M NO MAN, AND
I'M NO UNDERTAKER.
I AM DEATH, AND THAT
GRAVE'S A KINDNESS I
DON'T OFTEN GRANT.

THIS DUEL? ALSO
A KINDNESS. NEVER MIND
THE ONE-SIDEDNESS. YOU'RE
BEING GIVEN A CHANCE.

YOUR SECOND.
WHICH IS TWO MORE
THAN MOST EVER GET.

NOW DRAW.
YOUR.
GUN.
I'VE GOT A
JOB TO DO.

SWOOOOOOO......

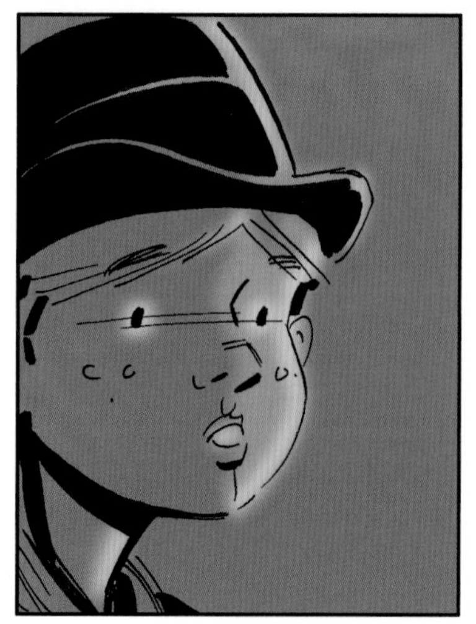

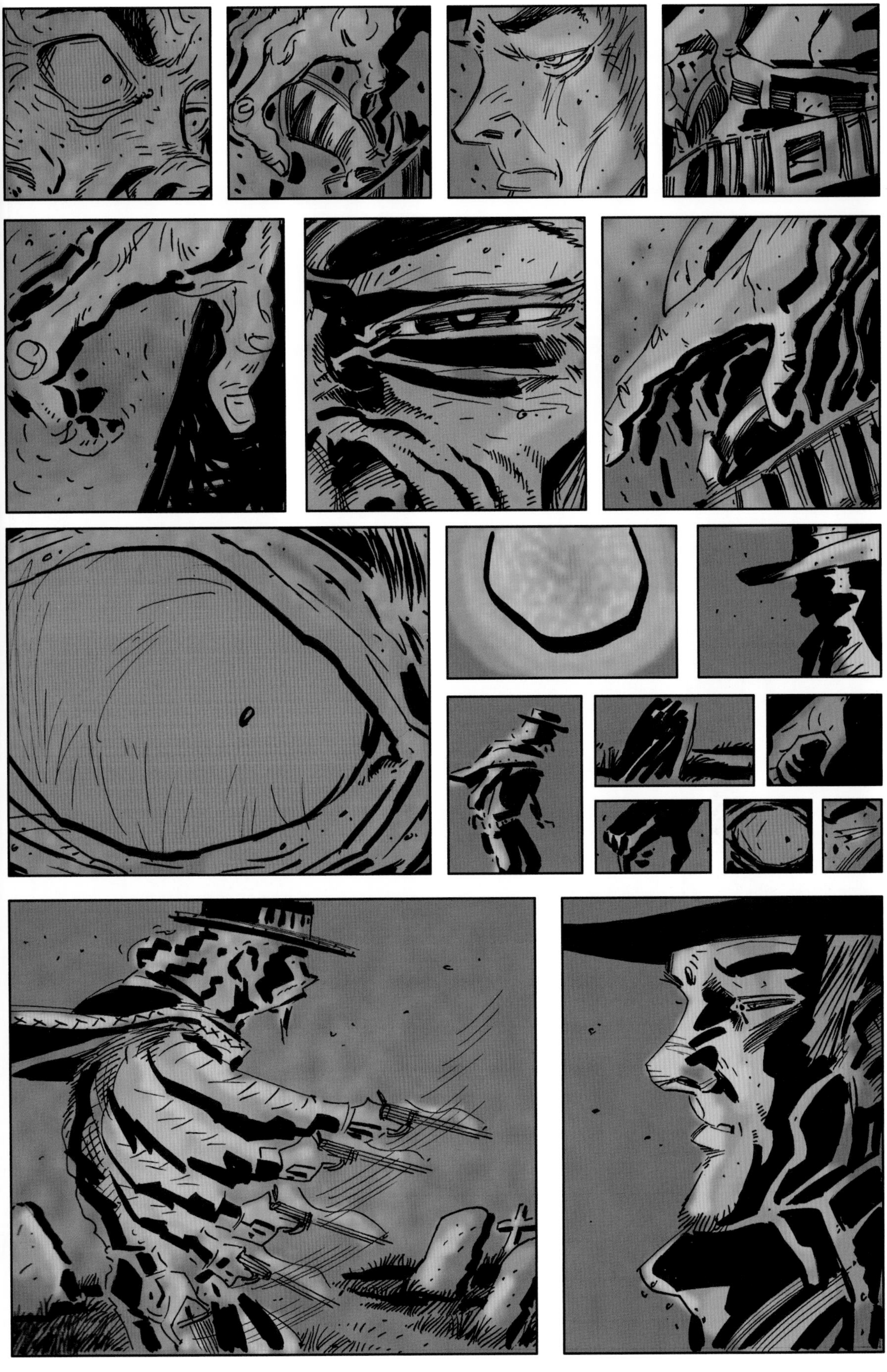

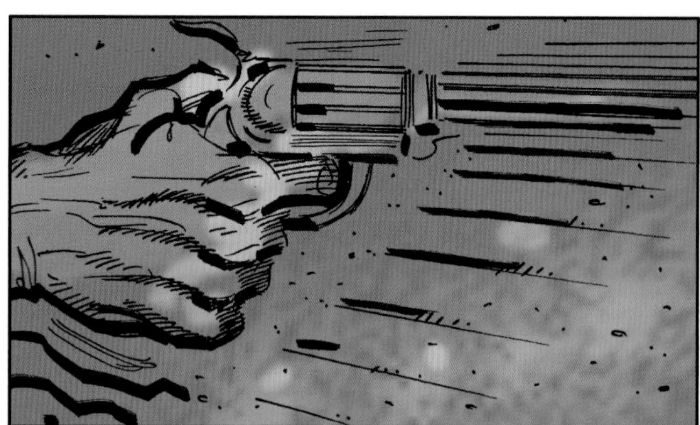

CLICK!

HUP!

BLAM!

BAT!

WHUMP!

BAT.

BAT!
BAT!

BAT.

A-HEH.

WASN'T HIS TIME. THAT'S WHY MY BULLET DIDN'T HAVE BUSINESS WITH HIM.

FAIR ENOUGH.

LET'S KEEP IT THAT WAY.

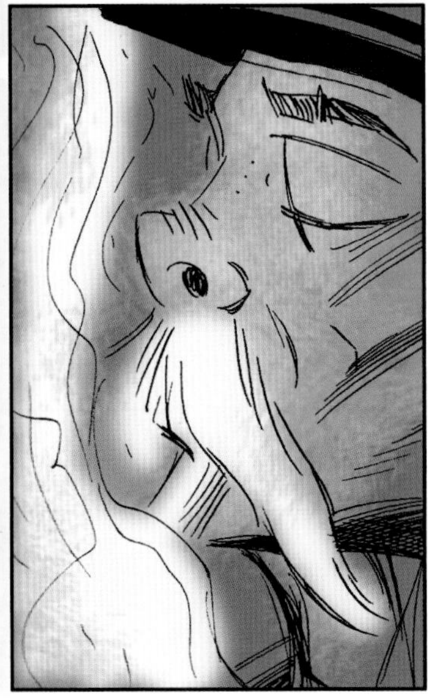

...HE DEAD?

SHOOT'M AGAIN!

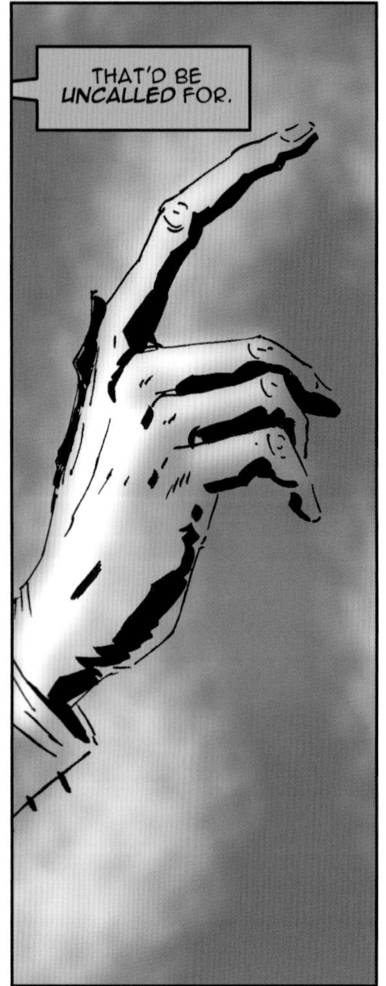
THAT'D BE *UNCALLED* FOR.

YOU CAN CONSIDER OUR BUSINESS ON HOLD.
"FOR NOW," I RECKON.
FOR NOW, YOU RECKON RIGHT.

THAT HUSK OF YOURS WON'T LAST FOREVER.
IT'LL WEAR OUT, AND WEAR DOWN, EVENTUALLY.

WHEN IT DOES, YOU'LL SEE ME AGAIN.
SURE AS TAXES.

AIN'T IT, "SURE AS..."

OH.
YEAH.

WELL, LOOK ON THE BRIGHT SIDE.
WHICH IS?
THATAWAY.

AND I'M NOTHING IF NOT A MAN OF MY WORD.

END.

BIVENS

ABOUT THE AUTHORS

Josh Hechinger is a Cancer who shares a birth year with Mega Man. He likes long walks, coffee, and Chinese food. He dislikes spiders, pizza, and the 22-page floppy. His favorite color is green, his favorite band is *Los Campesinos!*, his favorite film is *Kiss Kiss, Bang Bang*, and his favorite book is *The Long Goodbye* by Raymond Chandler. He lives roughly $6.50 away from Philly.

His other comics include *Bouncing Off Clouds* (with Matthew Humphreys) in Image's *Comic Book Tattoo*, and *Bear Beater Bunyan* (with Jorge F. Muñoz), available on iTunes and Google Android from Robot Comics.

Marvin Perry Mann began his comics career inking *The Trouble With Girls* (Malibu Graphics). After a departure into furniture-making and 3D modeling and animation, he returned to comics in 2002, digitally producing a 240-page silent comic strip and two flipbook animations for *Pause and Effect: The Art of Interactive Narrative* (New Riders). He is the artist and co-creator of four original graphic novels published by Archaia: *The Lone and Level Sands*, *Some New Kind of Slaughter*, *The Grave Doug Freshley* and *Inanna's Tears*. He lives in California.